SIXTY-FOURTH HONOR LECTURE
DELIVERED AT THE UNIVERSITY

A basic objective of the Faculty Association of Utah State University, in the words of its constitution, is:

> to encourage intellectual growth and development of its members by sponsoring and arranging for the publication of two annual faculty research lectures in the fields of (1) the biological and exact sciences, including engineering, called the Annual Faculty Honor Lecture in the Natural Sciences; and (2) the humanities and social sciences, including education and business administration, called the Annual Faculty Honor Lecture in the Humanities.

The administration of the University is sympathetic with these aims and shares, through the Scholarly Publications Committee, the costs of publishing and distributing these lectures.

Lecturers are chosen by a standing committee of the Faculty Association. Among the factors considered by the committee in choosing lecturers are, in the words of the constitution:

> (1) creative activity in the field of the proposed lecture; (2) publication of research through recognized channels in the field of the proposed lecture; (3) outstanding teaching over an extended period of years; (4) personal influence in developing the character of the students.

William A. Wilson was selected by the committee to deliver the Annual Faculty Honor Lecture in the Humanities. On behalf of the members of the Association we are happy to present Professor Wilson's paper.

Committee on Faculty Honor Lecture

On Being Human:
The Folklore of Mormon Missionaries

by
William A. Wilson

64th Faculty Honor Lecture
Utah State University
Logan, Utah

© 1981 Utah State University Press

On Being Human:
The Folklore of Mormon Missionaries

by
William A. Wilson*

Not long ago I was asked to entertain some of my colleagues at a faculty gathering by telling stories about J. Golden Kimball, that crusty old Mormon divine who salted his sermons and public statements with a liberal sprinkling of cuss words and earthy metaphors. Because I know a fair number of these stories and enjoy telling them, I agreed. The event was a tolerable success. At least most people laughed, and no one threw brickbats. Still, as I drove home, I wondered if I had not done more harm than good. I had, I feared, simply strengthened the notion, held by many, that the study of folklore might provide interesting material for after-dinner speeches but certainly could not be expected to increase our understanding of the human condition.

This evening I would like to rectify that impression. The night I told J. Golden Kimball stories I played the role of folklore performer. Tonight I will play the critic. My argument will be that the performance of folklore—whether it provides us with delight and amusement or causes us to fear and tremble—is one of our most fundamental human activities. The study of folklore, therefore, is not just a pleasant pastime useful primarily for whiling away idle moments. Rather, it is centrally and crucially important in our attempts to understand our own behavior and that of our fellow human beings.

To defend this thesis I will share with you some of the insights my colleague John B. Harris and I have gained from studying the folklore of Mormon missionaries. Some ten years ago Professor Harris and I began collecting missionary folklore, mostly from recently returned missionaries attending Brigham Young and Utah State Universities. The

---

*Professor, Department of English and Department of History; Editor, *Western Folklore*.

results of our efforts now fill eleven volumes—a data base large enough, we believe, to at last warrant some generalizations. I would prefer to move directly to a discussion of this data, but I have learned from past experience that if we hope to arrive at any common agreement tonight, we must first come to some general understanding of what folklorists study.

In brief, they study people, the "folk," who in face-to-face interactions with other people attempt to control the circumstances of their lives by generating, performing, and transmitting "lore," by communicating, that is, through traditional forms ranging from the songs they sing and the stories they tell to the ways they celebrate their birthdays and prepare their food.

The people who generate, perform, and transmit this lore are, among others, you people in the audience tonight. When the term *folklore* was coined in 1846, the "folk" were thought at that time to be unsophisticated, unlettered peasants—the *vulgus in populo*—people living mainly in rural areas, isolated from the more civilized members of society and carrying in their collective memory survivals, or relics, of earlier, primitive customs and usages. This notion held sway throughout the nineteenth century and through much of this one; indeed, it has not yet completely faded. For many the term *folklore* still conjures up images of European peasants spinning tales of olden times or of Appalachian hillbillies strumming happily away on their banjos.

By mid-century, however, most folklorists had begun to hold a more realistic view. They came gradually to understand that folklore can help us understand not just the past but also the present, that folklore can flourish in urban industrial centers as well as in the agrarian countryside, and that all of us—sophisticated and unsophisticated alike—possess folklore and participate in folklore processes. As a result, they began to speak not of *the folk* but of different *folks*, that is, of different folk groups isolated from the rest of society and bound together by such circumstances as age, occupation, religion, ethnicity, and regional habitat. And they began to study such diverse groups as children and senior citizens, airline hostesses and medical doctors, Amish and Catholics, westerners and southerners—and even such people as Mormon missionaries, who could be defined as an occupational subgroup within the larger Mormon religious group.

Though certainly an advance over the older view of the folk as peasants or quaint rural people, this newer concept, which dominates much of American folklore research today, is not without problems. First, it stereotypes people, failing to take into account differences and assuming that what is true of one group member will be true of them all. Second, it focuses on what is unique to a particular group rather than on what members of the group share in common with other people. As a result, folklore study, which above all else ought to be a humane discipline, fails at times to acknowledge our common humanity and serves, or can serve, as a divisive rather than a uniting force in society.

To counter these problems some folklorists have begun to speak not of different folk groups but of different social identities. For example, I am a Mormon; but I am also a father, a teacher, a Democrat, an Idahoan, a tennis fan, a photography nut, and so on. To assume that one can know me fully simply by identifying me as a Mormon is to assume too much. It seems safer to say that in certain situations my Mormon identity will become dominant and my other identities will be forced into the background, though never fully suppressed—that is, even in my most intense Mormon moments I will not cease entirely to be a Democrat, and conversely, when I play the role of Democrat, I will not cease to be a Mormon. In those situations in which my Mormon identity becomes dominant, I will think and act in traditionally prescribed ways, in ways somewhat similar to those in which other Mormons will think and act when their Mormon identities are dominant. This being the case, one should be able to observe these Mormon ways of thinking and acting and then say something about the nature of Mormon behavior in general. Generalizations, however, must be used with care; no one individual will ever fit the generalized pattern completely, and this behavior, though it may have taken on a distinctive Mormon coloring— or, in our case, a Mormon missionary hue—may not be peculiar to Mormons or missionaries at all but rather to people everywhere.

From this point of view, Mormon missionaries are not uniquely missionaries. Each is a composite of the identities he has brought with him to the field; no two are exactly alike. However, unlike the rest of us, who are constantly changing roles (and therefore identities), missionaries play the same role for the duration of their missions. Occasionally, and often to the displeasure of their leaders, some of the missionaries' other identities will come to the fore; but for the most part, from the time they are called to the field until they are released two years later, these young people are engaged full tilt in missionary activity. Even in those moments when they are not directly involved in proselyting efforts, they must at all times, day and night, be accompanied by at least one other missionary companion, a circumstance that reminds them constantly of their missionary role. They thus afford us an excellent opportunity to observe the behavior of people whose shared identity persists for a sustained period and to discover what is unique and what is universal in that behavior.

Presently some thirty thousand missionaries, most between the ages of nineteen and twenty-three, serve in all areas of the free world and in some not so free. One could argue that the geographical spread of these missionaries and the cultural differences in the lands in which they serve preclude the development of a folklore widely known to most of them. Such an argument overlooks the nature of missionary work. Though in the past this work was somewhat loosely organized and missionaries, once called to the field, were left pretty much to their own devices, this is not the case today. The work is now tightly structured and highly programmed and routinized. Missionaries in Japan, Finland, Argentina, and Los Angeles will follow essentially the same schedule, participate in the same activities, and abide by the same rules as missionaries throughout the system. Though regional differences will obviously occur, it is possible to identify a missionary lifestyle that has produced a common folklore.

This folklore has evolved over time from day-to-day interactions of missionaries facing similar problems and involved in similar social situations. As they have participated in typical activities (such as "tracting" [going from door to door] or holding discussions in the homes of investigators), or as they have experienced recurrent events (such as facing hostile crowds or witnessing some people accept their message and join their church), they have developed somewhat similar responses and attitudes to the circumstances of their lives, and they have told stories and participated in activities which embody these attitudes and which give them a sense of control in a world not always friendly. The more they have told these stories and participated in these activities the more they have formularized them into recognizable patterns. As they have continued to face problems and find themselves in social situations similar to those that have occurred in the past, they have sought resolutions in these now traditional stories and activities—or, in other words, in their folklore.

No matter what form this folklore takes—song, tale, customary practice—the performance of it will almost always be an act of communication, an act through which the performer attempts to persuade the audience, and sometimes himself, to accept a certain point of view or to follow a certain course of action. These performances might be called exercises in behavior modification. They may entertain us, but they also change us.

Obviously, not all communicative acts aimed at persuasion are folklore. We can distinguish those which are by at least three identifying features that "frame" them, or set them off, from the regular flow of communication.

First, folklore is framed by the use of beginning and closing markers. When we hear someone say, "Once upon a time . . ." or "Say, did you hear about . . . ," we know that regular conversation is about to be interrupted by the telling of a tale. When the narrator says, "And they lived happily ever after" or "And that really happened," we know that the telling has ended and that regular discourse will begin again. The markers that signal the beginnings and endings of other folkloric communications may be subtler, but they nevertheless exist; when we pick up the appropriate signal, we know what will follow.

Second, folklore is framed, as I have already noted, by a recurrent and clearly recognizable structural pattern. For example, the basic structure of Mormon legends of the Three Nephites is this: someone has a problem; a stranger (usually an old man) appears; the stranger solves the problem; the stranger miraculously disappears. A story may have more to it than this—the person visited may be tested by the old man before being helped—but it must have these elements. Any story incorporated into the Nephite cycle will be adjusted to make it conform to this pattern. The process is similar to a writer's attempt to develop his or her personal experience into a short story. To be successful the writer must distort the experience to make it fit the requirements of form. Missionaries telling their own experiences do the same thing. The experiences are real enough, but the missionaries must distort, or at least carefully select, the details of these experiences to make them fit the narrative forms traditional in the mission field.

Third, stories are framed by a stylized manner of performance. Stylistic devices include such things as gestures, body language, rhythmical speech, musical sounds, shifts in intonation, and the use of ceremonial language. When someone tells a J. Golden Kimball story and imitates Kimball's high-pitched nasal voice, the performer is using a stylistic device.

Folkloric communication, then, can be distinguished from other forms of communication by beginning and closing markers, by recognizable structural patterns, and by stylized presentation. These distinguishing features, of course, warrant our calling folklore what literature itself is generally considered to be—an artful rendering of significant human experience. In at least one important way, however, folklore differs from literature. No matter how much advice a poet may get from colleagues and no matter how he or she attempts to shape the lines to communicate effectively with a specific audience, once the poem is completed and committed to print, the exchange between poet and audience ends. Each person may respond differently to the poem and may interpret it differently. But the words themselves, as they appear on the printed page, will ever remain the same.

With folklore there is no printed page. There is only the performance in which a song is sung, a tale told, a ritual enacted. The song, tale, or ritual are parts of the whole, but they are not the whole itself. The performance is the whole. The markers I have discussed above do not set off *a* story; they set off the *telling* of a story, a telling whose form and meaning are shaped by teller and listener alike as each responds to and gives feedback signals to the other. Thus in a very real sense the telling *is* the tale, the singing *is* the song, the enactment *is* the ritual. The artistic tensions that develop as one reads a poem occur primarily between the reader and the lines on the written page and only indirectly, through these lines, between the reader and the poet. The artistic tensions that develop in a folklore performance occur directly and dynamically between listener and performer. We can record part of the performance and print it in a book as a folklore text, but in doing so we give readers only a mutilated bit of reality. The real art of folklore and the real meaning of folklore lie only in the performance of folklore.

For example, when a group of missionaries is faced with a problem that needs solving—what to do, for instance, with a recalcitrant missionary who will not do his duty or who may have committed an unworthy act— one of the missionaries will assume the role of storyteller, or performer. Looking to the wisdom handed down from the past and therefore considered to be of special value, he will begin to tell of an earlier missionary who behaved in a similar way and suffered the wrath of God as a result.

His listeners may not know the particular story being told, but they will know its form and will recognize the values the teller is attempting to uphold. They will expect him both to stay within the narrative bounds dictated by tradition and at the same time to perform well enough to excite their sympathies and persuade, or attempt to persuade, them to accept his point of view. In other words, they will judge the competency of his performance. As they do so, they will send back signals as feedback. He will then adjust his storytelling accordingly, manipulating the form and especially the style of his presentation to make it as artistically powerful, and therefore as persuasive, as possible. If he is successful, he will reform the sinner, or at least he will persuade fence-sitters not to follow the sinner's example. As we skim rapidly over a number of examples tonight, we should remember that behind each of them lies this kind of performance.

Clearly, no two missionary folklore performances will ever be the same, even if the same story is told in both. The time and place of telling, the nature of the audience, the skill of the teller, the reason for telling—all these will combine to make the form and meaning of each performance unique to that performance. Still, while each performance is different from every other one, each is also similar to others. From performance to performance, through time and space, there will be consistencies and continuities in the products of these performances (the stories, songs, customs, and language usages), in the ways missionaries express themselves, and in their reasons for doing so. These are the focus of our study.

To understand the significance of these consistencies and continuities in the lives of missionaries, we must look closely at the circumstances under which missionaries generate folklore and especially at the uses to which they put it. In the time remaining, I should like to look at four of these. Each is different from the others, but in each we find missionaries attempting to maintain a sense of stability in an unstable world.

The first use missionaries make of folklore is to create an esprit de corps, a sense of solidarity among themselves. When a brand new nineteen-year-old missionary, a "greenie," arrives in some distant mission field, frightened, feeling very much an outsider, and wondering if he should catch the next plane home, the first folklore he is likely to encounter will probably be directed against him. For example, in Norway, when a new missionary arrived, seasoned elders (missionaries):

> sat him down in a chair; they fixed a light above him, and they interrogated him about his moral life. When he volunteered the information that he had kissed a girl before, they let him know that he was completely washed up as far as his career goes in the mission. He would always be a junior companion, never be allowed to lead a discussion. And he believed the whole thing.

In London, England, new missionaries were told to save their bus-ticket stubs for a half penny rebate per ticket. The greenies saved drawers full of these—some, following instruction, even ironed them—only to learn later that they were totally worthless. In Texas a senior companion instructed his new junior companion how prayers were to be offered in the mission:

> "Now, Elder, out here we pray an awful lot. If we had to repeat these prayers all the time we'd spend most of our time on our knees and never have time to do the Lord's work. Instead, we have all the prayers numbered." With that the two slid to their knees and the senior volunteered to say the prayer. "Number 73," he prayed, and jumped into bed, leaving the new missionary in a crumpled mass on the floor.

In Norway a senior companion, after going through essentially this same ritual, prayed, "Lord, number 10 for me and number 35 for the greenie." In Spain greenies and senior missionaries prepared to eat a first dinner together:

> The zone leader asked one of the older elders to say the blessing on the food. They all bowed their heads, and the elder very seriously said, "Number nine, Amen." While the poor new missionaries were still recovering from that, the zone leader looked at the elder who had said the prayer and just as seriously retorted, "Elder, you always say the same prayer."

Sometimes church members, posing as someone else, usually an investigator, have joined the senior missionaries in these pranks. In Norway again, the missionaries asked a greenie:

> "Do you have your first discussion?" And he said, "I have it. I've been studying it. I learned it when I was down in the mission home." And they said, "Okay, you've got to have it good, 'cause we're giving it tonight." So they went—four of them—over to this

8

house to give it—the discussion. And, of course, it wasn't really an investigator; it was a member. And they said, "This man is very musically inclined, and it gets a little bit mundane talking to him all the time. He likes us to sing him the discussions." And so they started out singing the first two lines of the first discussion, and then said, "Hit it!" And so the new elder proceeded to sing the rest of the first discussion in Norwegian.

In California a senior companion offered to demonstrate to his new greenie how he succeeded in placing Books of Mormon in people's houses. The two of them knocked on a door. A woman answered, and the senior companion threw a book past her into the house and then ran, leaving the greenie to stammer out an explanation to the irate woman. The woman turned out later to be the bishop's wife "and all worked out right in the end." In Germany:

> A senior companion had a married friend who was coming through Germany on his honeymoon. He was just about to get a greenie, so he arranged a party with all the missionaries in the district to welcome him. He also arranged to have his married friend act as a companion to another missionary at the party. At the party they arranged to have the greenie find the supposed missionary kissing a girl, who in reality was his wife. They didn't tell the poor greenie that it was a joke until he had been on his knees in fasting and prayer for three days.

I could continue this way for the rest of the evening. The easiest missionary folklore to collect is this kind of prank played by seasoned missionaries, sometimes in collusion with members, on naive, unsuspecting greenies. When we first began to uncover these practices, we seriously wondered about the dedication of "ministers of the gospel" who would participate in such frivolous activity. Then a couple of our informants taught us what we should have known all along. One of them, a fellow who had protested to us that no such pranks had ever been played on him during his mission, later came to Professor Harris's office, laid his head on the desk, and sobbed, "I was never really a part of the missionaries; now I know that I had no jokes played on me because I was not accepted." Another young man told me that when he arrived in the Philippines, the first meal he was served in the mission home was made up of all green food served on green dishes on green linen to remind him of his greenness. "I felt like I had been baptized," he said. And this is exactly what these pranks are—baptisms, or initiation rituals. The missionary who had never been accepted by his fellows had not been initiated. People who must work closely together, who must depend on each other in a common struggle against an alien world, must, if they are to succeed, develop a camaraderie and a sense of community. Through the initiation, the new missionary, the outsider, is incorporated into the system. In scriptural terms, he puts off the old man, the greenie, and puts on the new man, the seasoned elder. He now belongs. He is first abused in some way; through the abuse he is humbled; as he recovers from the experience, usually through shared laughter, he becomes one with the group. "I felt kind of dumb at first," said one greenie, "but it was kind of fun after it was all over." Another commented, "It took me a while to cool down, but afterwards we laughed for days about the whole thing." Still another, who had been subjected to praying by numbers, said, "It took me a minute to figure it out, but after I did they all laughed and had a [real] prayer. We did it a few weeks later to some new elders." In this last instance the new missionary, only just initiated himself, soon began to initiate others and thereby was brought still more tightly into the system. Most missionaries participate in these pranks, then, as a means of establishing and maintaining a sense of community among their members.

Other folklore practices also contribute to this sense of community. A greenie newly arrived in the field will often hear his companions speaking a language he does not understand. A junior companion is not just a junior companion—he is "little brother," "the young one," "boy," "the slave." The senior companion, on the other hand, is "the boss," "the pope," "the chief," "sir." The girl back home is "the wife," "the lady in waiting." The rejection letter from this girl is "the Dear John," "suitable for framing," "the acquittal," "the Bix X." The mission home is "the zoo," "the Kangaroo court." Investigators are "gators," "our people." Good investigators are "goldies," "dry Mormons." Investigators who are not interested in the message but like to talk to missionaries are "professionals," "gummers," "lunchy," "the punch and cookie route." The Book of Mormon is a "bomb" (BOM). Baptisms are "tisms," "dunks," "splashes," "payday." Tracting is "bonking on doors," "self-torture." The tracting area is "the beat," "the jungle," "the war zone." Good missionaries are "spiritual giants," "rocks," "nails." Aspiring missionaries are "straight-arrow Sams," "cliff climbers," "pharisees." Bad missionaries are "screws," "hurters," "leaks," "liberals." The mission president is "the man," "Big Roy," "the head rhino." A returned missionary is "a reactivated makeout," "an octopus with a testimony." And so on. No missionary, of course, will know all of these terms. But almost all will know some of them or others like them. They have been generated over time as missionaries have characterized the circumstances of their lives in specialized language—in missionary slang or argot. When we asked missionaries why they used this language (and they use it most when they are by themselves—never with investigators and seldom with mission leaders), the most common response was that it creates a feeling of self-identification with other missionaries. It contributes, in other words, to that sense of community the initiation pranks help to establish. Once a greenie learns it he no longer is a greenie, an outsider. He is now a missionary. He belongs. He speaks the language.

But this is not the only use of this language. The second most common response to our question was that the language was a means of letting off steam, a kind of "silent rebellion." One missionary replied, "It was about the only thing we could say that wasn't programmed." In this unprogrammed language, spoken in casual conversations, missionaries have found a means of dealing at least in part with pressures imposed by the system. A missionary who can laugh at his beat-up bicycle ("the meat grinder"), at his food ("green slop"), at his apartment ("the cave"), and even at chafing rules is likely to be much more effective than one who broods over these circumstances. If he can laughingly call his tracting area "the war zone," he is likely better to survive the battle.

Sometimes, however, the laughter makes nonmissionary Mormons uncomfortable. Many of them do not particularly enjoy hearing the Book of Mormon referred to as a "bomb" (How many bombs did you place today, Elder?); nor do they like to hear baptisms called "splashings" or "dunkings." But these people do not have to see their names on a comparative list each month showing the number of books placed, and they do not have to struggle to meet a baptismal quota. The missionaries are simply dealing with pressures in one of the ways open to them—by smiling through language at what might otherwise be their undoing. It is quite clear from our data that most missionaries admire the good elders, "the giants," and dislike the bad ones, "the screws." Yet for the missionary who never quite succeeds as well as he would like, who never leads the mission in baptisms, it is sometimes comforting to view those who do as "climbers" or "straight-arrow Sams." Similarly, when a small group of missionaries refer to the mission president as "Big Roy" instead of "President Jones," they are not setting out to overthrow the authoritarian structure of the mission; they are simply reminding themselves that the authority who presides over them—fearsome as he sometimes appears—is also a man.

The second way missionaries use folklore, then, is to cope with the pressures resulting from submitting to the way of life and to the sometimes nagging rules prescribed by mission authorities. This fact is even more evident in some of the stories missionaries tell. Consider the following:

> Two missionaries were stationed in Zambia (formerly Northern Rhodesia) and were doing their normal missionary work. After a while they decided to split and take off into the Congo. Their chapel was only forty miles from the Congo, and Leopoldville, where all the revolutionary excitement was going on, was not much further away. So they devised a plan—to make out their weekly reports to mission headquarters two weeks in advance and give them to their landlady, who in turn would send one in each week at an appointed time. By this means, the missionaries would have two free weeks to venture into the wilds of the Congo. All this would have gone well, except the stupid landlady sent the report for the second week in first and the report for the first week second. That spilled the tomatoes, and the mission president caught them.

This is one of the most widely told stories we have collected. The details can change. The landlady can send all the reports in at once to save money. The place the elders visit will depend on the mission; from Brazil they go to Argentina, from Chile to the Easter Islands, from Italy to Egypt, from Norway to Scotland, from Germany to Yugoslavia, from Okinawa to Hong Kong, and from parts of the United States to other parts of the United States. In all cases, however, the structure is the same: the missionaries prepare activity reports for several weeks in advance and leave them with the landlady; the missionaries take an unauthorized trip; the landlady sends the reports in out of sequence (or all at once); the missionaries are caught.

In somewhat similar stories missionaries enter a sporting event against mission rules—a surfing contest, an auto race, a ski race, a bronco ride—and win. They are photographed; the pictures are published by the press; and the mission president sees them. In still others, missionaries participate in an event outside mission boundaries, like a World Series game, and somehow manage to appear in front of a TV camera just as their mission president back home sits down to watch the evening news.

Though many missionaries disapprove of the actions in these stories, most enjoy the stories. One of them said he enjoyed the mixed-up-report narrative "because missionaries don't do that kind of thing, and these guys did." That's exactly the point. Good missionaries do not do what characters in the stories do. Yet they delight in telling the stories. Why? Again, the missionaries themselves provide answers. One of them, who had been an assistant to his mission president told me, "Those of us who were straight, who kept the rules, had to tell stories like these to survive." Another assistant to a mission president said, "You would always like to do something like that yourself, and you kinda admire someone who has the guts to do it." A third missionary, in what is also a good description of a story-telling performance, commented perceptively:

> This [an unauthorized trip story] was told to me as a true story by my first companion while we were out tracting one day. If you spend eight hours a day just walking around knocking on doors, you gotta have something to do, and it's nice weather and you wish you weren't doing it [tracting], and you start telling stories. It's escapism. It took a long time; he embellished it and dragged it out so we could waste a lot of time with it. Then we'd daydream and think about where we'd like to go if we took a vacation.

In other words, some missionaries tell these stories because the characters in the stories do for them what they cannot do for themselves—take a vacation, at least in fancy, from the rigorous life they must pursue each day of their missions. The characters in the narratives do not, I should stress, provide models for the missionaries to emulate. Most missionaries know that to behave in such a way would be destructive to both themselves and the missionary system. The wayward missionaries in the stories, as Roger Abrahams has suggested of other such trickster heroes, are not models for conduct but rather "projections of desires generally thwarted by society." The trickster's "celebrated deeds function as an approved steam-valve for the group; he is allowed to perform in this basically childish way so that the group can vicariously live his adventures without actually acting on his impulses." In other words, as one of our missionaries said, "The elders told stories like this just to relieve the monotony, so you could just imagine what it would be like without getting in trouble for [doing] it."

The third way missionaries use folklore is to persuade themselves and their companions to conform to accepted standards of conduct. Through dramatic narrations which tell of God and Satan intervening in their lives, missionaries attempt to show what punishments will befall the erring and what rewards await the righteous. The message of the unauthorized trip stories we have just considered is ambiguous. Since the wayward elders are always caught, the narratives could be told to warn missionaries to stay in line. Sometimes they are. Normally, however, like trickster tales in general, they are told as amusing stories, as stories designed to provoke laughter. The accounts of supernatural punishments and rewards, on the other hand, are told in dead seriousness.

For missionaries who dishonor their priesthood and engage in sacrilegious acts, the wrath of God is quick and sure. One widely known story, recounted throughout the mission system, tells of elders who, as in the following account, are struck dead for testing their priesthood power by attempting to ordain a post or a coke bottle or an animal: "Two missionaries were messing around, and they decided to confer the Priesthood on a dog which they saw on the street. Before they could complete the ordinance, a bolt of lightning came and struck the dog and the two elders, and it *zapped* them."

Ironically, it is usually Satan rather than God who punishes the missionaries for their wayward conduct. In one rather terrifying cycle of stories, a missionary attempts to strengthen his testimony of Christ by seeking first a testimony of Satan. In Denmark, much to the horror of his companion, a missionary began one night to pray to the Devil.

> He proceeded to pray, hour after hour; his companion had gone to bed and left him on his knees praying for a manifestation, or wanting to see the devil in person. And so, as the story goes, he finally . . . made enough noise so his companion woke and went to the window and saw a black figure on a black horse coming down the road toward their apartment. And they were up

at least two stories, and this particular individual, as the story goes, jumped out of the window.

Another telling of the story, this time from Norway, ended this way:

> He looks over to the bed where his companion has gone to bed finally, and he's completely dead from his appearance, and there's a black figure on a white horse in the room, who is laughing. And then it just kind of fades away, until there's nothing and the companion's dead.

In many tellings of the story, the nonpraying companion summons the mission president for help. Usually when they enter the room by breaking down the door, they find the praying elder suspended in air, his hair sometimes as white as an old man's. In one account, when they open the door, the suspended elder's body is slammed against the wall, instant death the result. In another, they find the bed pinned to the ceiling with the missionary dead between bed and ceiling. In still another the elder is in bed, burned from one end to the other. In some instances the shell of a body remains, but the insides have been cooked out.

Since not many missionaries are likely to pray to the Devil, these stories are probably told and retold because of their evocative and symbolic power. They can be seen as warnings against evil in general. Numerous stories, however, do relate to specific missionary rules and regulations and are told to inspire proper adherence to them. For example, a photograph taken of an elder swimming, against mission rules, showed a black figure hovering near the swimmer. A Brazilian missionary refused to sleep in his temple garments because of hot weather: "When his companion woke in the morning, he found the errant elder pressed into the wall so hard that he could hardly pull him off. The elder was obviously dead from being mashed into the wall." In Oklahoma two missionaries, one with a broken arm, attended a fundamentalist revival against mission rules. The preacher healed the missionary's arm, but as a result the elder was possessed by an evil spirit. When the mission president cast out the spirit, the elder's arm broke again. In other stories, missionaries are either killed or tormented for violating a variety of rules: experimenting with spiritualism, playing the ouija board, swimming, boating, dating a girl, playing rock music, arguing with companions, not staying with companions, or sometimes simply not working hard enough. In actual performance, these stories have an emotional impact I cannot begin to communicate here. I have listened to them, and they have frightened me. Missionaries who participate in the telling or hearing of them will not lightly violate mission rules.

If the missionaries' God is a wrathful God, he is also a generous God, amply rewarding those who do his will. Stories demonstrating this point are so numerous I cannot begin to survey them here. Three brief examples will have to suffice.

> Two missionaries in the Canadian Mission were driving home from a discussion meeting one day, and there was quite a bad storm going. They were clear out in the middle of nowhere when their car broke down, and they were unable to repair it. They decided they would just freeze to death if they stayed there, so they got out of the car and started walking down the road. After a couple of hours they were pretty badly frozen anyway, and could tell they weren't going to be able to go much farther. Just then they heard a car coming behind them. It stopped and the man opened the door, and they got into the back seat. They were so cold they just laid down on the floor, and didn't even look at the man. Finally they came to a service station, and the man stopped the car at the side of the road and let them out. They got out and stumbled over to the station, but they still hadn't really got a look at the man in the car. When they got up to the station, the attendant looked surprised, and asked where they had come from. They said from the car that had just stopped out in front. He said, "There hasn't been any car come along for a couple of hours." They went out to the road and looked, but there weren't even any tire tracks. [The man driving the car was thought to be one of the Three Nephites.]

> There were two elders who were tracting, and one woman invited them into her home and said she was looking for a true church. And she fed them. They made an appointment to come back and teach her some time later. As soon as they came back, and she saw who they were at the door, she invited them in and said, "I want to be baptized," without even talking to them. And they asked her why, and she said that she had read that the true servants of the Lord could eat poison things and they would not be harmed. And then she told them that what she had fed them last week had been poison.

A missionary and his companion one time decided to take a little bike ride through the countryside, and they just kept going and going and going, and got farther out into the country. And finally they came to this little farm. It was so late that they couldn't leave, so the couple were very, very, very nice, and in fact, they even vacated their own bed and gave it to him and his companion, and they slept on the floor. And as it turned out, they were converted—the whole family.

The first two stories deal with the very real dangers missionaries face on the highways and at the hands of the frequently hostile people they must try to convert. The telling of these stories provides some relief from the fear engendered by these circumstances. For example, the teller of the missionaries-in-the-storm narrative related it to prove "the ability of the Lord to protect those who place their faith in him and live good lives." The teller of the poison story, a mission leader, used it "as a faith-promoting experience of what can happen if elders honor their priesthood and do their jobs properly." The message of both is clear: do your duty and the Lord will protect you. The third narrative belongs to a category I call last-door stories. In these, missionaries are led to, or are impressed to knock on, just one more door, behind which always lives a future convert. Again the message is clear: no matter how discouraged you are, no matter how many doors have been slammed in your face, if you will trust in the Lord, keep trying, and knock on that last door, you will eventually succeed.

All of the stories we are considering here—whether of punishments or rewards—follow what I call an anxiety-reducing formula. In the performance of such a story, the narrator will "name," or identify, a recurrent problem (a missionary who seems possessed by an evil force, for example, or a hostile community that threatens the safety of the missionaries); the performer will seek in the traditional stories available to him accounts of similar problems solved in the past; applying the wisdom gleaned from these stories, he will suggest a behavioral resolution to the present difficulty (don't break mission rules or work hard and trust the Lord). Missionaries who participate in such performances will have their fears allayed, will gain a sense of control over a threatening environment, and will thus be able to work more effectively.

The final use to which missionaries put folklore is one that in some ways subsumes all the others. In this instance, missionaries tell stories to persuade themselves that, in spite of massive evidence to the contrary, they may eventually emerge victorious. The largest number of narratives here are the conversion stories I have just alluded to, stories that tell of missionaries bringing converts into the church and that provide hope to so-far unsuccessful elders. But in many narratives the missionaries do not win converts; they just win—they get the best of a hostile world that has seemingly conspired against them. For example, a missionary who has been tormented again and again by animals will delight in the following account:

> He went to this discussion. The lady's cat was always bothering him. This cat just kept coming in and would attack everything on the flannel board [the board missionaries use for demonstrations]. He came up close to him and this elder just kinda reached down and flicked it on the bridge of the nose. Didn't mean to hurt the cat but it killed it. It dropped on the floor and the lady was out of the room at the time, so they curled it around the leg of the chair. And he sat and petted it all through the rest of the discussion. The next time they went, the lady mentioned the cat was dead.

Most of these stories have to do with missionaries getting the best of smart alecks they encounter while tracting. For example, when a jokester says, "I hear you guys believe in baptism by immersion," and throws a bucket of water on the elders, one replies, "Yeah, and we also believe in the laying on of hands," and then he "cools him." When a nosy lady snickers, "I hear you Mormons wear secret underwear," a sharp elder responds, "Well, isn't *your* underwear secret?" Or "Ma'am, there's nothing secret about our underwear. If you'll show us your underwear, we'll be willing to show you ours." When a redheaded Norwegian woman fumes, "I know what you guys do. You come over here to get all the women and you take them back to Salt Lake City and sell them," the missionary replies, "That's right. We just sent a shipment off last week. In fact, we had ten with red hair, and lost one dollar a piece on them." When a woman asks the missionaries at her door if it is true that all Mormons have horns, the new junior companion replies:

> "Yeah, as a matter of fact I just had mine clipped in Salt Lake just before I came out here." And she says, "Really?" and he says, "Yeah, you can feel the little bumps right here on my forehead."

> And so she put her hand on his forehead, "Well, I don't feel anything." And he said, "Not even a little bit silly?"

In one instance that recalls the story in which missionaries were poisoned as a test of their power, two missionaries called on a protestant minister.

> He said, "Gentlemen, I have here a glass of poison. If you will drink this poison and remain alive, I will join your church, not only myself but my entire congregation." And he said, "If you won't drink this poison, well, then I'll conclude that you are false ministers of the gospel, because surely your Lord won't let you perish." And so this put the missionaries in a kind of a bind, so they went off in a corner and got their heads together, and they thought, "What on earth are we going to do?" So finally, after they decided, they went back over and approached the minister and said, "Tell you what—we've got a plan." They said, "You drink the poison, and we'll raise you from the dead."

In these stories the missionaries gain victory over their adversaries through the skillful use of their own wits. In other stories, when the opposition is keener, they are not equal to the task and are forced to bring the Lord in to fight the battle for them. In these accounts, following biblical example, the elders shake dust from their feet and thereby curse the people who have treated them ill. The Lord responds to the missionaries' actions in a dreadful manner. In Norway a city treats missionaries harshly; they shake dust from their feet, and the city is destroyed by German shelling during the war. Throughout the world, other cities that have mistreated missionaries suffer similar fates. Towns are destroyed in South America by wind, in Chile by floods, in Costa Rica by a volcano, in Mexico by an earthquake, in Japan by a tidal wave, in Taiwan and Sweden by fire. In South Africa a town's mining industry fails, in Colorado a town's land becomes infertile, and in Germany a town's fishing industry folds. Individuals who have persecuted missionaries may also feel God's wrath. An anti-Mormon minister, for instance, loses his job, or breaks his arm, or dies of throat cancer. A woman refuses to give missionaries water and her well goes dry. A man angrily throws the Book of Mormon into the fire only to have his own house burn down. In one story, widely known, two elders leave their garments at a laundry, and when the proprietor holds them up for ridicule, both he and the laundry burn, the fire so hot in some instances that it melts the bricks.

I do not admire the sentiments expressed in these stories, but as a former missionary who has been spat upon, reviled, and abused in sundry ways by people I only wanted to help, I understand them. I still remember standing on doorsteps after being stung by cruel, biting rejections, and muttering to myself, "Just wait, lady. Comes the judgment, you'll get yours." I would not have "dusted my feet" against anyone; few missionaries would. But many savor the victories which are theirs when they participate in performances of these stories, performances which persuade them that God is on their side and will help them carry the day. For a moment at least the world bent on thwarting their intentions to save it seems conquerable.

In one of our stories a newly arrived missionary goes into the bathroom each morning, lathers his face richly, and shaves with great care. His companion, growing suspicious, checks the razor and discovers the greenie has been shaving without a blade. In a missionary song, a parody of "I am Sixteen Goin' on Seventeen," a senior companion sings to his greenie:

> You are nineteen, going on twenty
> Now greener than a lime,
> And you have learned the 12 discussions
> If you are on the dime.
>
> Totally unprepared are you
> To face the world of men,
> Timid and scared and shy are you
> Of things beyond your ken.
>
> You need someone older and wiser
> Telling you what to do.
> We are twenty-one, some of us twenty-two.
> We'll take care of you.

In studying missionaries we must keep always in mind that we are dealing with untried, indeed often unshaven, young men—nineteen and twenty—who in their first real encounters with the outside world are placed in circumstances that would try the mettle of the best men. In spite of J. Golden Kimball's quip that the church must be true, otherwise the missionaries would have destroyed it long ago, these young people function remarkably well. Few of them crack under the enormous pressure they face each day.

I am not foolish enough to argue that the missionaries endure only because of their folklore. They endure primarily because they are committed to their gospel and convinced of the importance of their work. But that conviction is constantly bolstered and maintained by the lore they have created. As we have seen, through the performance of this lore they develop a strong esprit de corps; they relieve the pressures imposed by the rule-bound nature of the system; they channel behavior down acceptable paths; and, most important, they develop a picture of a world that can be overcome.

That world, of course, is very often the world missionaries want it to be rather than the one it is. A performance of folklore is much like a game. In it missionaries create a world similar to but nevertheless separate from the one in which they live. And in that fictive world they play the roles and face the problems which will be theirs in the real world. If the performance is successful, the fictive world and the real world for a moment become one, and missionaries leave the performance with the belief, or at least the hope, that problems faced and solved there can be faced and solved in similar ways in real life. They are a little like the ballad hero, Johnny Armstrong, who, mortally wounded, leaned on his sword and shouted encouragement to his men:

> Saying, fight on, my merry men all.
> And see that none of you be taine;
> For I will stand by and bleed but awhile,
> And then will I come and fight again.

Missionaries bleed. But they come back to fight again. The significance of folklore performance is that it helps them keep up the fight.

In all this there is nothing unique to Mormon missionaries. The problems faced by missionaries are not just missionary problems; they are human problems. A missionary who tells a new junior companion to save worthless bus-ticket stubs is not much different from a boy scout who sends a tenderfoot on a snipe hunt or a logger who crams a greenhorn's lunch bucket full of grasshoppers. The world is full of greenies who, to function adequately, must first be initiated. Other people besides missionaries, then, must develop a sense of community, must deal with pressures imposed by the systems they live under, must encourage proper behavior, and must come at last to believe they can subdue the world. What missionaries share with others is not so much common stories or practices but rather common reasons for performing them—common means of achieving these ends. From studying the folklore of missionaries, or railroaders, or college professors, we will, to be sure, discover what it means to be a missionary, a railroader, or a college professor. But if we learn to look, we will discover also what it means to be human.

Selected Bibliography

All folklore cited in this paper comes from the Harris-Wilson Missionary Collection, Utah State University Folklore Archives.

A full bibliographic survey of the rich sources lying behind the ideas presented here is beyond the compass of this paper. The following selections have helped shape my thinking and will serve as a good beginning for one wishing to pursue the subject further.

Abrahams, Roger D. "The Complex Relations of Simple Form." In *Folklore Genres*, ed. Dan Ben-Amos, pp. 193-214. Austin and London: University of Texas Press, 1976.

———. "Folklore and Literature as Performance." *Journal of the Folklore Institute* 9 (1972) :75-94.

———. "Introductory Remarks to a Rhetorical Theory of Folklore." *Journal of American Folklore* 81 (1968) :143-158.

———. "Some Varieties of American Heroes." *Journal of the Folklore Institute* 3 (1966) :341-362.

———. "Toward an Enactment-Centered Theory of Folklore." In *Frontiers of Folklore*, ed. William R. Bascom, pp. 79-120. American Association for the Advancement of Science, Selected Symposium 5. Boulder, Colorado: Westview Press, 1977.

Bauman, Richard. "Verbal Art as Performance." *American Anthropologist* 77 (1975) :290-311.

Ben-Amos, Dan. "The Context of Folklore: Implications and Prospects." In *Frontiers of Folklore*, ed. William R. Bascom, pp. 36-53. American Association for the Advancement of Science, Selected Symposium 5. Boulder, Colorado: Westview Press, 1977.

———. "Toward a Definition of Folklore in Context." *Journal of American Folklore* 84 (1971) :3-15.

Dundes, Alan. "Who Are the Folk?" In *Frontiers of Folklore*, ed. William R. Bascom, pp. 17-35. American Association for the Advancement of Science, Selected Symposium 5. Boulder, Colorado: Westview Press, 1977.

Georges, Robert A. "Conceptions of Fate in Stories Told by Greeks." In *Folklore in the Modern World*, ed. Richard M. Dorson, pp. 301-319. The Hague and Paris: Mouton, 1978.

———. "Feedback and Response in Storytelling." *Western Folklore* 38 (1979):104-110.

———. "Toward a Resolution of the Text / Context Controversy." *Western Folklore* 39 (1980):34-40.

———. "Towards an Understanding of Storytelling Events." *Journal of American Folklore* 82 (1969):313-328.

Jones, Michael Owen. "Prologue," "Section Introductions," "Epilogue." In *Foodways and Eating Habits: Directions for Research*, vi-xii, 1-3, 41-44, 91-93, 134-137. Special issue of *Western Folklore* 40 (January 1981).

———. "Bibliographic and Reference Tools: Toward A Behavioral History." Paper read at the Folklore and Local History Conference, New Orleans, 5 September 1980.

Toelken, Barre. *The Dynamics of Folklore*. Boston: Houghton Mifflin Co., 1979.

———. "The 'Pretty Languages' of Yellowsman: Genre, Mode, and Texture in Navaho Coyote Narratives." In *Folklore Genres*, ed. Dan Ben-Amos, pp. 145-170. Austin and London: University of Texas Press, 1976.